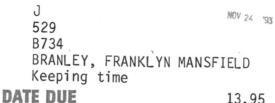

Keeping Time

Keeping Time

From the Beginning and into the 21st Century

Franklyn M. Branley
Illustrated by Jill Weber

Houghton Mifflin Company
Boston 1993

Library of Congress Cataloging-in-Publication Data

Branley, Franklyn Mansfield.
  Keeping time / Franklyn Branley ; illustrated by Jill Weber.
    p. cm.
  Summary: Describes the different ways in which we measure time.
  ISBN 0-395-47777-8
  1. Time — Juvenile literature. 2. Time measurements — Juvenile
literature. 3. Clocks and watches — Juvenile literature.
4. Calendar — Juvenile literature.   [1. Time measurements.
2. Clocks and watches. 3. Calendar.]   I. Weber, Jill. ill.
II. Title.
QB209.5.B69   1993   92-6783
529 — dc20   CIP
              AC

Printed in the United States of America
VB 10 9 8 7 6 5 4 3 2 1

Contents

1. We Live by the Clock — And by the Sun

Many people will celebrate December 31, 1999, as a very special New Year's Eve. The next year will be 2000, so these people will believe they are marking the end of the 20th century and the start of the 21st. But they will be one year too early. The year 2000 is the last year of the 20th century. The 21st century begins on Monday, January 1, 2001.

The calendar used most widely throughout the world began with the year 1. There is no year zero. This means that the year 2000 is the last year of the present century.

There is bound to be confusion about this. Many people will be convinced that the year 2000 marks the start of a new century, and they will not be persuaded otherwise.

The story of time is full of many ideas such as this, some of them a lot harder to understand than the date when one century ends and a new one begins.

One of these is time itself. What is time? Certainly it regulates our lives, for you and I live by the clock.

When people lived on farms, the clock was not very important. People got up with the sun, milked the cows morning and evening. They worked in the fields until the sun was high in the sky. Then they had lunch and rested. Once more they worked, continuing until the sun was low in the sky.

There were no electric lights to change night into day, so bedtime came with the approach of darkness.

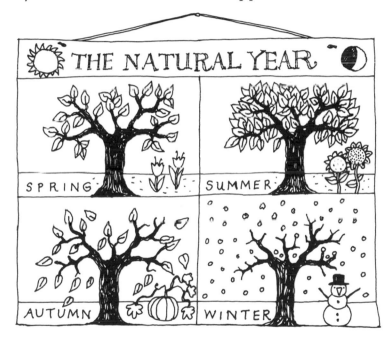

People had natural ways to keep track of time. The changing seasons, with the blossoms of spring and the snows of winter, marked the passage of a year. The motion of the sun across the sky determined their daily activities.

The sun, moon, and stars were timekeepers for early people. Farmers lived close to the soil and to their animals; they just knew the time of day, the seasons of the year, the passage of time. They needed no clocks.

Today, everyone needs clocks. People have busy schedules in which minutes and even seconds become important. Airplanes, buses, and trains take off at specific times. If they didn't, things would get mixed up for sure. You can say that clocks keep the world operating.

The sun still gives us our idea of what time it is. But to know the exact time, we must use a clock. Keeping accurate time became more and more important as people moved from farms into cities and as they traveled farther and farther.

In this book we will find out how people learned to keep track of time and how to measure it.

First, let's see what time is. Is there a beginning of time? or an ending? It depends upon how you measure it.

Suppose it is Monday, January 1, 2001, the beginning of the 21st century. According to this system of measuring, time began two thousand years ago, in the year 1.

But some people believe that time began 3761 years earlier. This, they say, was the year of creation. Great events have occurred in the history of different groups of people, so important that time is measured from a specific date — the birth of a savior or of a great leader, for example. When you think of it this way, time has many beginnings.

Astronomers think of the beginning of time in another way. They say that time began at the beginning of the universe. There are good reasons for believing that the universe began 15 billion years ago.

Ever since, the universe has been expanding. So time has been moving forward; the universe has been getting older. It is expected that the universe will go on expanding, perhaps forever. So time will continue on and on.

THERE WAS A GREAT EXPLOSION! IT WAS THE START OF THE UNIVERSE & THE BEGINNING OF TIME

You and I are not really concerned with this idea of time. Still, time is something we use every day of our lives. For young people, time may seem to last forever — there's always enough time, and lots more of it. Older people are more aware of the limits of time.

So we have several answers to our question about the beginning of time. There may be many beginnings. Is there an *end* to time? There is for the lives of people. For the universe, there may be no end. It may go on forever, down through eternity.

Andrew Marvell, an English poet in the 1600s, wrote:

But at my back I always hear
Time's wingèd chariot
            hurrying near;
And yonder all before us lie
Deserts of vast eternity.

2. How to Make a Sundial

We can tell time, just as people did long ago, by the changes that take place around us — especially the changes in the length and direction of shadows. In the early morning, the shadows of trees and houses are long and they fall toward the west. As the day

EARLY MORNING
the shadows are
the longest

NOON
the shadows
are the shortest

progresses, the shadows become shorter. They are shortest at noon. At the close of the day the shadows are long once more. In the afternoon, shadows fall toward the east. This all happens because the sun rises, moves across the sky, and sets. You can see these changes yourself by watching the shadows of a building, a tree, or a pole.

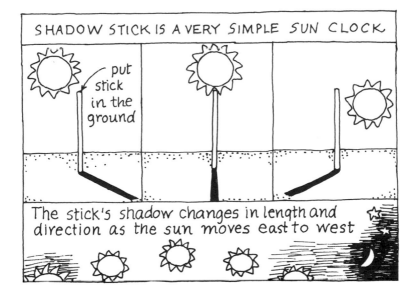

SHADOW STICK IS A VERY SIMPLE SUN CLOCK

put stick in the ground

The stick's shadow changes in length and direction as the sun moves east to west

HOW TO MAKE A SUNDIAL

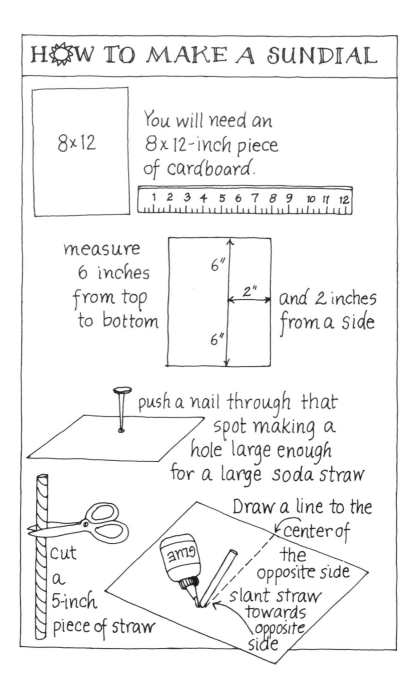

8x12

You will need an 8x12-inch piece of cardboard.

1 2 3 4 5 6 7 8 9 10 11 12

measure 6 inches from top to bottom

6"

2"

6"

and 2 inches from a side

push a nail through that spot making a hole large enough for a large soda straw

Cut a 5-inch piece of straw

glue

Draw a line to the center of the opposite side

slant straw towards opposite side

Put your sundial outdoors on a flat surface where sunlight falls on it. When it is noon by the clock (1:00 P.M. if you are on daylight saving time), turn the cardboard so that the shadow of the straw falls along the line you drew. This will be a north-south line. The straw will point toward Polaris, which is the North

Star. (The line will be exactly north-south only on the first day of spring and fall. At other times of the year, it will be close to a north-south line.)

Fasten your sundial in place with tacks if you can. Notice how the shadow of the straw changes in length and direction as the day goes by. Each hour, mark the position of the shadow along the edge of the cardboard and write in the time: 8:00, 9:00, and so on. Draw lines from the straw to the marks. In the following days, you can tell time by the position of the shadow.

The straw is the gnomon of your sundial. The word *gnomon* comes from a Greek word meaning "one who knows" — a gnomon "knows" the time.

You may want to make another sundial using a piece of stiff cardboard. You can copy these three parts, perhaps making them twice the size shown here. If you know about making models, you can use balsa wood or a plastic sheet.

Sundials enabled people to keep track of time a bit more accurately than by simply watching the moving shadows of objects. The entire history of timekeeping is a record of efforts to make it more precise.

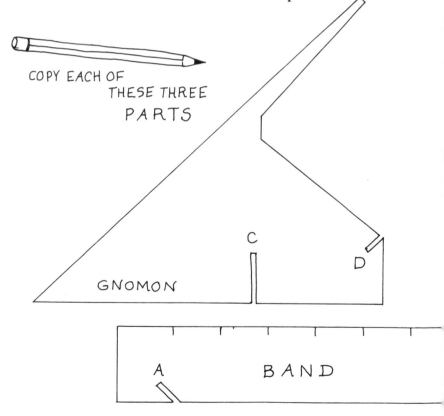

COPY EACH OF
THESE THREE
PARTS

GNOMON

C

D

A   BAND

TO ASSEMBLE:

1. Place the gnomon on the base matching C slots

2. Then place the band on the base and gnomon matching A's, B's, and D

Place so this point heads toward Polaris

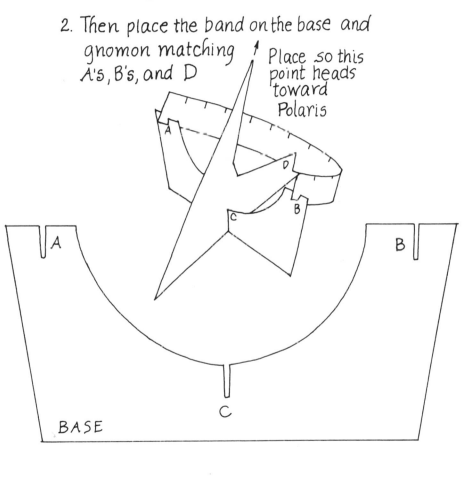

A

D

C

B

A

B

C

BASE

B

3. Does a Sundial Give Correct Time?

Changing shadows give us some idea of the time. With a sundial we can measure the movements of the shadows and so tell time a bit more accurately. But adjustments must be made to sundial readings to make them agree with other timekeepers, such as clocks.

Clock time is related to sun time, but the two are not exactly the same.

From one noontime by the sun, which is the moment when the sun has reached its highest location for that day, to the next noon is a solar day — a day by the sun.

From noon by the clock to the next noon is a clock day. During a year, a solar day may be a few minutes shorter or a few minutes longer than a clock day. The sun reaches the highest location in the sky a few minutes early or a few minutes late by the clock.

Also, clocks keep the same time within an entire time zone. The sun moves constantly, so when it is at the noon position for you, places a few miles east of you have already had noon. Places a few miles west of you have not yet had noon. To avoid the confusion that this arrangement caused, it was decided in 1884 that the world would be divided into time zones, each about 1000 miles wide. All places within the zone would have the same time.

This means that a place at the eastern edge of a time zone has noon by the sun one clock hour before a place at the western edge. That's another reason why solar time and clock time do not agree. So, when using your sundial, don't be surprised if it is out of step with your clock.

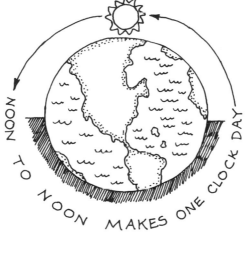

NOON TO NOON MAKES ONE CLOCK DAY

4. Other Kinds of Timekeepers

People learned to tell time quite well using sundials. But sundials are no help at night, indoors, or on cloudy days.

The sun is a pretty good timekeeper because it moves across the sky at a regular interval. In all good timekeepers, something must happen at regular intervals.

Candle Clock

Many different timekeepers have been invented. One is simply a candle with lines drawn around it. An hour went by as the candle burned from one mark to the next. To determine what the space between marks should be, a sample candle may have been burned, starting at noon by the sun. After the sun had moved to the 1 o'clock position on the sundial, a mark was put on the candle. In some such way, people found the amount the candle would burn in 1 hour. A 6-hour candle would have six segments marked off. You can make your own candle clock to see how this was done.

HOW To MAKE A CANDLE CLOCK

1. Place 2 candles in holders and light one of the candles.

2. When one hour has gone by, make a mark on unlit candle.

3. Repeat until the lit candle is all gone.

4. Your clock is done.

Water Clock

Another kind of timekeeper used dripping water to measure time. You can make your own using a paper cup.

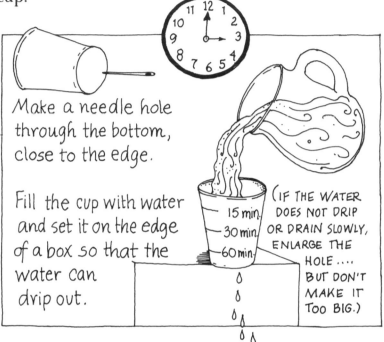

Make a needle hole through the bottom, close to the edge.

Fill the cup with water and set it on the edge of a box so that the water can drip out.

15 min.
30 min.
60 min.

(IF THE WATER DOES NOT DRIP OR DRAIN SLOWLY, ENLARGE THE HOLE ....
BUT DON'T MAKE IT TOO BIG.)

Start your water clock on the hour. Put a mark on the cup at the level of the water after 15 minutes, half an hour, an hour. Once you have done this, you can use your cup to keep track of time. Simply fill the cup again. As the water drains to the level of the marks, you'll have a 15-minute interval, half-hour, and hour. If you wish, you can measure the water in the cup you drain into. The results will be the same.

18

Ancient water clocks worked in a similar manner. The sun's motion was used to set the marks on the container.

EARLY WATER CLOCK

Water Alarm Clock

With a tin can, a ruler, and a simple water clock, you can make an alarm clock.

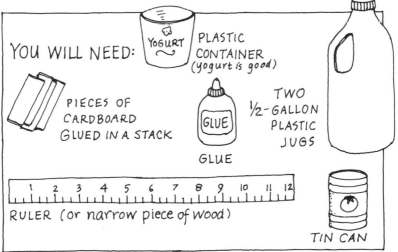

YOU WILL NEED:

PLASTIC
CONTAINER
(yogurt is good)

PIECES OF
CARDBOARD
GLUED IN A STACK

GLUE

TWO
½-GALLON
PLASTIC
JUGS

RULER (or narrow piece of wood)

TIN CAN

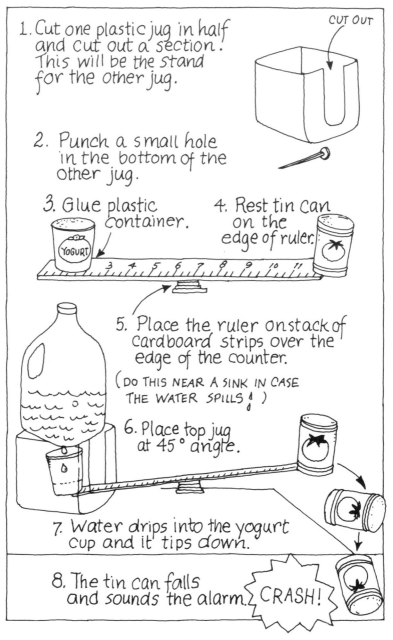

1. Cut one plastic jug in half and cut out a section. This will be the stand for the other jug.

CUT OUT

2. Punch a small hole in the bottom of the other jug.

3. Glue plastic container.

YOGURT

4. Rest tin can on the edge of ruler.

5. Place the ruler on stack of cardboard strips over the edge of the counter.

(DO THIS NEAR A SINK IN CASE THE WATER SPILLS !)

6. Place top jug at 45° angle.

7. Water drips into the yogurt cup and it tips down.

8. The tin can falls and sounds the alarm. CRASH!

Put a glass or two of water in the top container. The water will drip out. When there is sufficient weight, the container end of the ruler will go down and the tin can end will go up. The tin can will fall to the floor and make quite a racket.

You have made a water alarm clock.

You can set the alarm to any time you want by moving the cardboard stand, or you can add some weight to the tin can. You'll have to try different arrangements to set it to the time you want.

Early people may have made alarm clocks like this, using earthen pots.

Sand Clock

Instead of using water flowing from a container, you could use sand as an egg timer does. These timers are made of two glass globes containing fine, dry sand. A small opening connects the two globes. It takes 3 minutes for the amount of sand inside to run from one globe to the other, so you can make a three-minute egg — not too hard or too soft. Big timers like this are called hourglasses — the sand in them runs out in 1 hour. An egg timer can be called a 3-minute glass.

You can make your own sand clock using a plastic milk container and dry sand. The container and the sand must both be bone dry. Spread the sand on a newspaper on a sunny day. The sun should dry it out.

With a small nail, punch a hole through the bottom of the container. Put sand in the container and see if it runs out. If it does not, make the hole a bit larger. You'll have to experiment until the hole lets sand go through smoothly, but not too fast.

HOW THE SAND CLOCK KEEPS TIME

Place the container on a glass or jar so that the sand can run into it.

After every 15 minutes put another mark on it.

Once you have done this, you can use the sand clock to keep time.

15 min.

Sand clocks were made in various sizes. According to one story, the ancient Romans used sand clocks to time speeches given by politicians in the Senate. Most speakers were not very interesting, so the sand clocks got smaller and smaller.

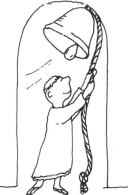

Clocks Are Invented

Sundials, sand clocks, and water clocks were awkward, and they demanded constant attention. Something mechanical was needed, something that could be started and would run steadily for some measured interval of time. The clock was the answer.

Clocks first came into use in Europe during the 13th century. Before that time, mechanical bells, the forerunners of clocks, were used in monasteries.

In monasteries, the monks pray several times during the day. A timer that rang a bell at regular intervals called the monks to prayer. The bellringer was modified to become a timekeeper, a clock as we know it. It is very likely that the first "clock" was used in 996 by Pope Sylvester II. (The word comes from the German *glocke*, or bell.)

Early clocks had one hand that turned around a dial, making one turn in 24 hours. The gears moved the hand evenly, so it kept pace with the daily movement of the sun. Early clocks were not very accurate and had to be corrected frequently.

Today we still have 24-hour clocks: the hour hand makes one turn in one day. Presently our day begins at midnight. It used to begin at noon. Before that, the day began at sunset. In some religions, the day still begins at sunset.

These different systems of keeping time were awkward for business and travel, so it was decided that the day should begin at midnight. The hours from midnight to noon would be called the morning hours — A.M., or ante meridiem, which means before the meridian. (When the sun is on your meridian, the line that goes from pole to pole and passes overhead, it is noon. So A.M. means before noon.)

The hours from noon to midnight are called the hours of the afternoon, or P.M. for post (after) meridiem.

The day was divided into two segments, each having 12 hours. Most clock dials are therefore marked off into 12 sections. The hour dial makes two complete turns in 24 hours.

In a mechanical clock, a power spring keeps it going. It also has smaller springs and gears that regulate the clock and keep it moving evenly. A digital clock has no springs or gears.

In the early 1800s, mill owners created the "mill clock." It could be made to run fast or slow depending upon how hard the people were working.

Digital Clocks

Digital watches contain a microchip, like those in a computer. The heart of the watch is a quartz crystal. A small electric current, supplied by the battery, makes the crystal oscillate, or vibrate. It oscillates at a steady 32,768 times a second. That means it can turn an electric current on and off that many times in one second.

The pulses are cut in half by a series of transistors, which are on-off controls. The first reduction is from 32,768 to 16,384. This is further reduced to 8,192, to 4,096, and so on to 1. The operation, completed in 15 steps, arrives at the interval of one second.

The passing of one second is shown on the digital display. This is usually a sandwich having a mirrored surface at the bottom and a clear plastic layer at the top. Between them is a layer of millions of liquid crystals that float freely. Scores of electric connections contact the layer of crystals. When a connection carries a current, the electricity causes certain crystals to line up, producing a display of numerals.

Digital watches are very accurate, and they can measure small fractions of a second. The interval they are based on is the frequency, or rate of vibration, of the quartz crystal — 32,768 times a second.

Atomic Clocks

The more vibrations there are in one second, the more accurate a timekeeper can be. An atomic device is the answer. A quartz clock is based on the action of molecules; an atomic timekeeper is based on the action of the electrons in an atom.

The core of an atom is surrounded by electrons located at various distances from it. The electrons move continually and change their distance from the core. They do this at a regular rate. For example, the outer electrons of a cesium atom change position precisely 9,192,631,770 times a second. An atomic timekeeper measures these changes, effectively dividing each second into that many parts.

Atomic timekeepers — or atomic clocks, as they are called — are accurate to one billionth of a second in 24 hours. That would be 365 billionths in one year, 36,500 billionths in 100 years. After a billion days, or some 2,740,000 years, the error would amount to only one second.

We have come a long way from sundials, hourglasses, and water clocks. We can measure time as precisely as we want to.

Keeping Time Even More Accurately

Navigators plotting the locations of ships and planes use time signals that are accurate to a millionth of a second: a microsecond.

The locations of space probes are accurate to a billionth of a second: a nanosecond.

The motions inside the nucleus of an atom are measured in picoseconds — trillionths of a second — or even in femtoseconds — one thousandth of a picosecond.

There are more femtoseconds in one second than there were seconds in the past 31 million years.

Time and tide wait for no man.

5. What Is Time?

We've been talking about time and clocks, but we haven't yet found out what time really is.

Time is something that can go by very slowly. When you are in a dentist's chair, it drags along. When you're having a good time, you want it to last and last. But, of course, it doesn't. Time goes by.

It goes into the past, which does not really exist, except in our memory. Tomorrow is the future. It doesn't exist either, except in our minds. The present is this moment — right now, as you are reading these words. Time goes by. But what is it?

The dictionary says: "Time is a limited interval between two successive events." That means very little

until you think about it. In a sand clock the event is the movement of sand from one container into another. In a water clock it is the flow of water. In a solar day, the events are the rising and setting of the sun. In a clock, the event is the motion of the hands around the dial. In a digital clock, it is the vibration of the quartz crystal. In a lifetime, the events are birth and death. In the universe, the first event was the Big Bang, the moment the universe was created. Ever since, the universe has been expanding; the clock runs on and on. It may do so forever.

We measure time by events. The basic measure, the one we have been using for centuries, is the movement of the sun. People have gotten used to solar days and to clocks. We get up in the morning. We work rapidly as the sun moves along. When the sun gets lower in the sky, we slow down. As the sun sets, our body rhythms make us more and more relaxed. We go to bed.

Although the sun seems to move across the sky, it actually does not. It is the turning of the earth that makes the sun appear to move. A single rotation is the basic interval we use for timekeeping. As the earth turns, we first see the sun low in the sky at sunrise; then we see it at the highest location, which is noon. Later, the sun is once more low in the sky.

So for most of us the earth is our clock. The time needed for it to turn around once is one day — our basic time unit.

As the earth spins, it also goes around the sun. As we move along, the sun appears to move from one part of the sky to another. The drawing on page 33 shows how this happens. When a journey is completed we have one year, another time unit.

31

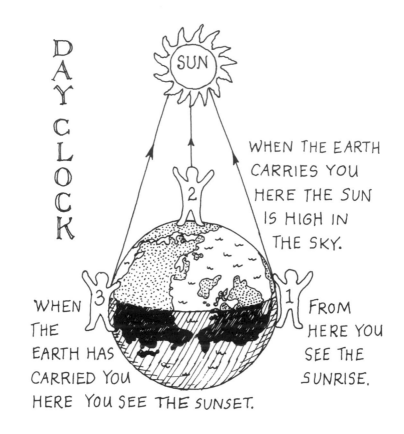

DAY CLOCK

SUN

WHEN THE EARTH CARRIES YOU HERE THE SUN IS HIGH IN THE SKY.

2

WHEN THE EARTH HAS CARRIED YOU HERE YOU SEE THE SUNSET.

3

1 FROM HERE YOU SEE THE SUNRISE.

The spinning of the earth gives us a day clock. The motion of the earth around the sun gives us a year clock.

Time is always something happening: sand and water flowing, clock hands moving, the earth spinning, the universe expanding, crystals vibrating.

One thing is certain: we cannot repeat yesterday, nor can we live in the future. The only real thing is this moment. Be sure you don't waste it.

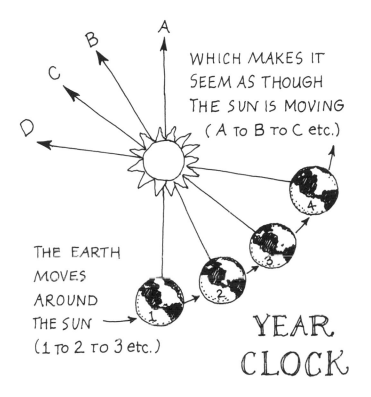

A
B
C
D

WHICH MAKES IT
SEEM AS THOUGH
THE SUN IS MOVING
(A TO B TO C etc.)

THE EARTH
MOVES
AROUND
THE SUN
(1 TO 2 TO 3 etc.)

YEAR
CLOCK

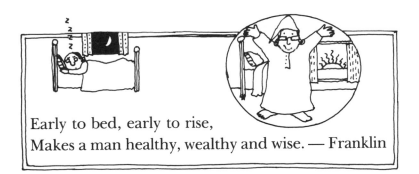

Early to bed, early to rise,
Makes a man healthy, wealthy and wise. — Franklin

6. Standard Time and Daylight Saving Time

People have learned what time is and how to keep time very accurately. They have also learned how to avoid a lot of confusion concerning timekeeping.

For example, until 1883 every town in North America had its own time. The clocks in each town were adjusted at noon, when the town's sundial showed that the sun had reached its highest position for that day. This posed no problem in earlier days, because people did not travel very much. When they did, they moved slowly by horse and wagon and without any definite schedule; they got to the next town quickly or slowly depending entirely upon the horse.

When trains ran from town to town, there had to be a timetable telling when the trains would arrive and depart. Whose time should be used in making the schedule? The time in towns only 100 miles apart might differ a quarter hour or more. This became very confusing for travelers. The confusion lasted from the early 1800s, when the railroads began to operate, until 1883.

Great Britain had had the same sort of problem. In 1880 it was decided that all of Great Britain should have the same time. Noon for the entire country would be when the sun was above the meridian that went through Greenwich, which is just outside London. That would be when the sun was at the highest location over Greenwich for that day. Seven minutes earlier the sun would have been over the meridian that passes through the eastern part of the country.

In another twenty minutes, the sun would be on the meridian passing through the western part of the country.

Noon by the clock, in all parts of Great Britain, would not be the same as noon by the sun. It still isn't, but all parts of the country have the same time by the clock.

On November 18, 1883, following a suggestion made by Sir Sandford Fleming, a Canadian railway engineer, the railroads in North America decided to follow the lead of Great Britain — though not exactly.

Because Canada and the United States extend so far east and west, it would have been awkward for all parts of the country to have the same time. Suppose noon for the entire country was when the sun was above the meridian that goes through Washington, D.C. The clocks on the west coast would then be reading noon long before the sun was high in their sky.

NOON

U.S. STANDARD TIME ZONES

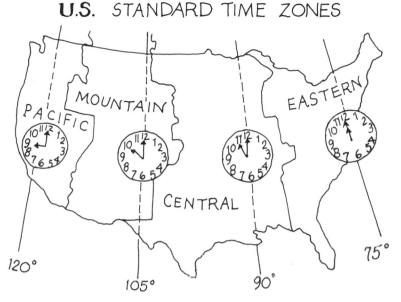

To avoid such an odd arrangement, the country was divided into four time zones: Eastern, Central, Mountain, and Pacific. The clocks on all trains within a time zone would all show the same time. They would not have to be changed every few miles to agree with the sun's position. Trains could travel several hundred miles east or west without changing the clocks. The clocks would be changed only when the train went from one time zone into another. Many cities adopted "railroad time" because the system avoided so many problems. A place at the eastern edge of a time zone might be as much as 1000 miles from a place at the western edge. By sun time, the difference between the two places would be 1 hour. By the clock, the time would be the same. It still is.

In 1884, people from several countries around the world met in Washington, D.C. They decided that the world should be divided into 24 time zones beginning with the Prime Meridian, the one that goes through Greenwich, England. Time by this method would be worldwide standard time, or simply standard time. Most countries accepted the idea (though not all of them). Twenty-four time zones were set up, one for

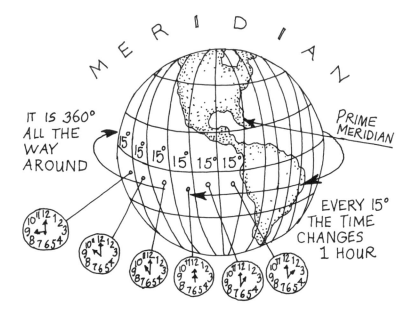

IT IS 360°
ALL THE
WAY
AROUND

PRIME
MERIDIAN

EVERY 15°
THE TIME
CHANGES
1 HOUR

each hour of the day. All the way around the earth is 360 degrees, so every 15 degrees (360 divided by 24) there is a change of 1 hour.

When it is Monday noon in Greenwich, the time at a place 15 degrees east of Greenwich would be 1:00 P.M., at 30 degrees it would be 2:00 P.M., and so on around to the 180th meridian, where it would be 12:00 midnight on Monday — 12 hours later than in Greenwich. The time 15 degrees west of Greenwich would be 11:00 A.M., at 30 degrees west it would be 10:00 A.M., and so on to the 180th meridian, where it would be midnight on Sunday — 12 hours earlier than in Greenwich. Obviously a place cannot have two different days at the same time. The problem is solved by changing the time at the International Date Line. To see how this is done, turn to page 77.

This system of changing the clocks 1 hour every 15 degrees is followed by most countries around the world. But there are exceptions, notably the People's Republic of China. China extends over some 50 degrees and so should have four time zones. But China has only one time zone. Noon is the moment when the sun is over the meridian that passes through

BEIJING

Beijing, the capital of the country. In western China, noon by the clock occurs several hours before the sun has reached its highest location in the sky for that region. This would be very confusing to a visitor.

Standard time was officially adopted in the United States in 1918, although it had been used informally during the previous thirty years.

Daylight saving time is a method of adjusting the hours of daylight so that there is more time in which we can be active outside or inside without using artificial lights.

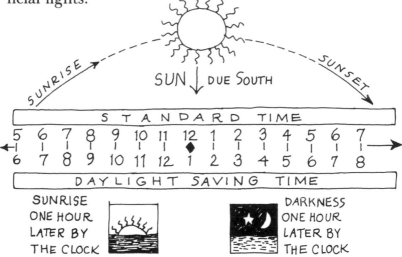

When we use daylight saving time, our clocks "spring ahead" in spring (we set them an hour ahead), and they "fall back" in the fall (we set them back an hour). When daylight saving begins, the first Sunday in April, we lose an hour of sleep. We gain an hour on the last Sunday in October.

Suppose the sun rises at 6:00 A.M. and sets at 6:00 P.M., and suppose you get up with the sun and go to bed with the sun. There would be 12 hours of daylight. With daylight saving time there would also be 12 hours of daylight, but you would get up at 7:00 by the clock (still 6:00 by the sun). You would go to bed at 7:00 by the clock (still 6:00 by the sun). The difference is that there is 1 less clock-hour in the morning when you are sleeping and 1 more in the evening when you are active.

The idea for daylight saving time started with Benjamin Franklin in 1784, when he was minister to France. While there he often went for a walk early in the morning. He noticed that people shuttered their windows and slept late in the morning, wasting the free morning light. In the evening they burned lamps and candles in order to keep active after the sky had darkened. Franklin said, Why not push the clock ahead an hour, then it would be light later in the evening. People would save money because they would burn fewer candles at night. They wouldn't need them during the dark early morning hours because they would be sleeping.

Little was done about daylight saving time, however, until much later. During the First World War, daylight saving time was used briefly in order to save energy. But after the war we abandoned the idea.

In the 1940s, during the Second World War, the plan was tried again. When the war ended, some places went back to the "old time" while others continued to use daylight saving time. Towns right next to each other could have an hour's difference in time. To avoid confusion, our government decided that the entire nation should have daylight saving time. The idea was not enforced, but most people agreed they wanted more daylight in the evening hours. If a state wished, however, it could decide not to adopt daylight saving time.

Today, almost the entire United States uses daylight saving time, starting on the first Sunday of April. There are a few exceptions: Arizona, Hawaii, and part of Indiana do not change their clocks. Farmers found it confusing and, as they point out, sheep, cows, and pigs don't change their "clocks." They decided it was better all around to stay with standard time.

7. Why Are There 24 Hours in a Day?

Whether we use standard time or daylight saving time, there are 24 hours in a day. But it wasn't always so. At the close of the 18th century, during the French Revolution, people used the metric system of measuring, which, as you know, is based on the number 10. They reasoned that the system should also be used for timekeeping and so introduced the 10-month year and the 10-hour day. There was some merit in the idea, but other than the convenience the metric system provided, there was little to recommend the 10-hour day, so it did not last.

There is nothing "natural" about the 10-hour plan. However, the 24-hour day is based upon the earth's rotation. In one day, the planet makes one turn. Therefore the sun appears to go once around the sky. It appears to complete a circle, which means it travels through 360 degrees.

The idea of 360 degrees in a circle goes back thousands of years to the Babylonians and Egyptians. The Babylonians were an ancient people in what is now Iraq.

These people used a counting system based on 6. They had 360 degrees in a circle (6 × 60); 12 months, each having 30 days. They marked a circle into 360 parts, matching the yearly circle of the sun around the earth. There was one part for each day of the year.

Egyptian and Babylonian days were divided into six periods, or watches: three from sunrise to sunset, three more from sunset to sunrise. Later, each period was shortened: there were six daylight watches and six in darkness, for a total of twelve.

In ancient days, astronomers who knew about the motions of the earth and the sun were also astrologers. People called on them to predict events by the position of the stars, sun, and planets at the moment of a person's birth. To be more exact when telling people how the stars and planets would affect them, the astrologers needed smaller time divisions. They made the twelve watches of the day into twenty-four.

The year of 360 days, the circle of 360 degrees, the division of a year into 12 months of 30 days each, and 24 hours in a day all fit into the old system of counting by sixes — each number is divisible evenly by 6.

The units of our timekeeping have become smaller and smaller, giving us greater and greater accuracy. Still, all are based upon natural events: the rotation of the earth and its yearly journey around the sun.

Time is something that keeps everything from happening at once.

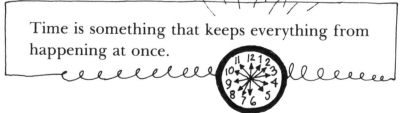

8. Why Are There 60 Minutes in an Hour, 60 Seconds in a Minute?

Most of us have little need for measuring time in seconds; minutes are close enough. The school bus may pick you up at twenty after seven: 7:20. But it could be a few minutes early or late; it would certainly be a few seconds one way or the other. There is no need to say that the bus will be there at twenty minutes, ten seconds, after seven: 7:20:10.

However, some events have to be measured in units smaller than minutes, so each minute came to be divided into 60 seconds. The division into 60 parts rather than 100, or any other number, is logical when you recall that a day was divided into 24 parts.

THERE ARE 360° IN A CIRCLE

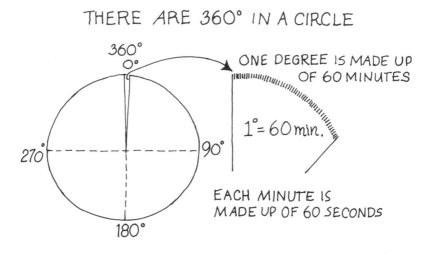

360°
0°
ONE DEGREE IS MADE UP OF 60 MINUTES

$1° = 60$ min.

270°   90°

EACH MINUTE IS MADE UP OF 60 SECONDS

180°

When it came to dividing those 24 parts into smaller units, the Babylonians' knowledge of a circle and its parts was also used. The circle-time connection came about because of the sun's motion. In one year, it appears to go all around the sky, completing a circle. A Babylonian year was 360 days long. In one day, the sun moved through 1/360 of its total journey. Each of these units is called a degree. (In a circle, as you know, there are 360 degrees.) Each degree is divided into 60 parts, called minutes, and each minute is also made of 60 parts, called seconds.

48

In one hour by the clock, the sun moves through 15°. In 24 hours it moves through 360°

15°

24 x 15 = 360°

In timekeeping we use similar divisions. We divide each hour into 60 minutes and each minute into 60 seconds. While the minute hand moves from one minute to the next, the second hand makes one complete turn: it moves through 360 degrees.

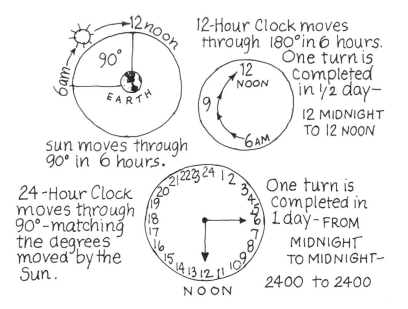

12noon

90°

6am

EARTH

sun moves through 90° in 6 hours.

12-Hour Clock moves through 180° in 6 hours. One turn is completed in ½ day—

12
NOON

9

6AM

12 MIDNIGHT TO 12 NOON

24-Hour Clock moves through 90°-matching the degrees moved by the Sun.

NOON

One turn is completed in 1 day – FROM MIDNIGHT TO MIDNIGHT—

2400 to 2400

While the hour hand moves from one hour to the next, the minute hand moves through 360 degrees — again, one complete turn. In half a day the hour hand also moves through 360 degrees. The entire cycle occurs twice each day on a 12-hour clock.

A 24-hour clock is geared so that the hour hand makes only one turn in 24 hours. On a 12-hour dial, only half a day is shown. On the 24-hour dial, a whole day is displayed, so the divisions on it are smaller. The display of minutes (and seconds) can be seen more easily on a digital clock.

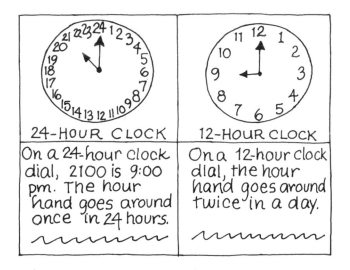

24-HOUR CLOCK	12-HOUR CLOCK
On a 24-hour clock dial, 2100 is 9:00 pm. The hour hand goes around once in 24 hours.	On a 12-hour clock dial, the hour hand goes around twice in a day.

Timekeepers have become more and more accurate, and they have become able to use smaller and smaller units. For example, operations that go on in the heart of a large computer take place in only billionths of a second.

9. How Long Is a Day?

The clock you and I live by, whether a 12-hour clock or one that records 24 hours, is set to keep mean solar time. The mean is the midpoint between the longest and the shortest. If you had five numbers — say, 2, 4, 6, 15, 20 — the mean would be 6. (Average is different. You find the average of the five numbers by adding them together and dividing by 5, giving 9.4.) Some solar days are longer than others. Because of this, clocks do not measure the length of solar days; they measure the length of a mean solar day.

As you know, our clock is based upon the turning of the earth. The earth is a clock, and the time unit is one complete rotation. If the earth always took the same time to make a rotation, there would be no problem. But it doesn't.

You can see why if you measure your own rotation. Face a picture on a wall, or a tree or pole. Then spin around once. When you face the same object again, you will have made one complete rotation.

SPIN AROUND ONCE

Suppose the object you lined up with was a car or bicycle or anything that was moving. When you finished making a turn, the object would be in a different place. You would have to turn a bit more to catch up with it.

That's what the earth does.

To measure the earth's rotation, the planet must line up with an object that does not change position, such as a star. (Stars are so far away that, even though they move, the motion cannot be noticed here on

Earth. For this purpose, we say the star stands still.)

To find a star-day — a sidereal day, as it is called — a location on the earth lines up with a distant star. The interval until the next sighting of the star is a sidereal day. It is 23 hours, 56 minutes, 4.09 seconds of mean solar time — time by a clock.

As you can see in the drawing, solar days are longer. During a sidereal day, the sun has moved a bit, so it takes a few minutes for the earth to catch up to the sun. A solar day is 24 hours long, but not always.

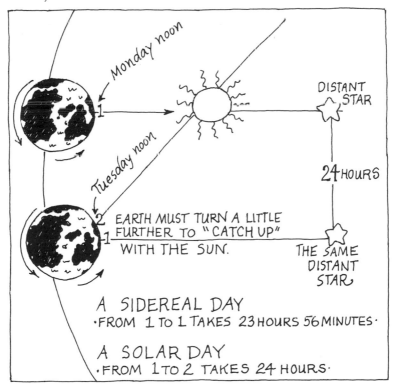

DISTANT STAR

24 HOURS

EARTH MUST TURN A LITTLE FURTHER TO "CATCH UP" WITH THE SUN.

THE SAME DISTANT STAR

A SIDEREAL DAY
·FROM 1 TO 1 TAKES 23 HOURS 56 MINUTES·

A SOLAR DAY
·FROM 1 TO 2 TAKES 24 HOURS·

In one year, 365 days, the sun moves once around the sky. That is, it moves through 360 degrees. That means each day it moves 1/365 of 360 degrees — just a little less than 1 degree. But that is not always true. For example, when the earth is close to the sun, in January, the sun moves slowly. Six months later, in July, the sun moves more rapidly. This means some solar days are shorter than others.

Aside from differences in the lengths of days caused by motions of the sun, the length of the day varies for other reasons.

Slight variations in the earth's rotation could not be measured until very accurate clocks were developed, instruments that could measure intervals as small as a few millionths or even billionths of a second. These superclocks have found that in a year the earth may be four or five thousandths of a second too slow or too fast.

Tides caused by the pull of the moon slow down the earth. Earthquakes may upset the motion, as do severe storms and movements of large air masses. The earth's surface is made of huge plates, often larger than continents, that are continually slipping and sliding, sometimes digging, under one another. The movements of such gigantic masses certainly affect the earth's rotation.

So, when you are asked what time is it, you can glance at a watch and give the answer. Or you can ask a few questions of your own. Do you want sidereal time or solar time? Actual solar time or mean solar time? Or, you may say, the tides are especially high today, so we expect that the earth is going to be a millionth of a second late.

For most purposes, the earth remains a fairly dependable clock. Its motions remain essential guides to timekeeping. But our best clocks are much more even and steady than the spinning earth.

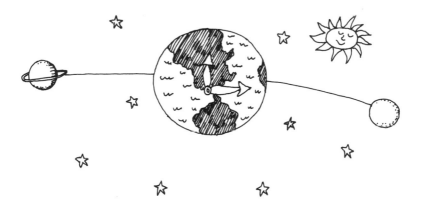

10. Why Are There Seven Days in a Week?

Time periods, such as the solar day, the solar year, and the lunar month, are based on natural motions of the sun and moon. There is no similar natural reason why there should be seven days in a week.

The moon goes through phases, changes in appearance, taking about one month to complete a cycle. Also, just about seven days are required for the moon to change from new to first quarter, another seven from quarter to full, seven more to the last quarter, and another seven days from the last quarter to new once more. Perhaps, as some people believe, the idea of a seven-day week came from this time interval. If so, the week is also natural, a time period based on events in the sky.

However, it is generally believed that the days of the week were introduced by astrologers. They connected the fortunes of people with the positions of the planets known at that time — Mercury, Venus, Mars, Jupiter, and Saturn — which wandered among the stars. The motions of the sun and moon were also observed, and came to be grouped with the five wanderers.

Astrologers believed that the day a person was born had a strong influence on that person's entire life, for each day was dominated by one of the seven gods who gave their names to the days of the week.

The ancient Romans, who were strong believers in astrology, called the days Dies Solis, Dies Lunae, Dies Martis, Dies Mercurii, Dies Jovi, Dies Veneris, and Dies Saturni. The English words we now use come from the Romans and from other peoples — the Saxons and Teutons who lived in Germany centuries ago. Their names for the days of the week were Sun's day, Moon's day, Tiu's day, Woden's day, Thor's day, Frigg's day, and Setern's day.

ENGLISH	LATIN	ANGLO-SAXON
SUNDAY	DIES SOLIS Day of the Sun	Sun's Day
MONDAY	DIES LUNAE Day of the Moon	Moon's Day
TUESDAY	DIES MARTIS	Tiu's Day
WEDNESDAY	DIES MERCURII	Woden's Day
THURSDAY	DIES JOVI	Thor's Day
FRIDAY	DIES VENERIS	Frigg's Day
SATURDAY	DIES SATURNI	Setern's Day

You can easily see which planets gave their names to Sunday, Monday, and Saturday. The other names look only somewhat like the names we use today.

Dies Solis is Latin for "day of the sun." The Teutons called it Sunnundag. In England the name gradually became Sunday. The German people call the day Sonntag; to the Dutch it is Zondag. The day was associated with Apollo, the sun god, called Helios, Sol, and Shamash in different languages. He was a most important god who rode in a chariot with golden wheels that was pulled across the sky by four white stallions.

The name Monday also comes to us from the early Teutons. Their important gatherings were held at the time of the full moon, so they used the moon as a timekeeper. They believed that a boy drove the moon chariot across the sky. Wolves chased him along and occasionally got close enough to take a bite. Sometimes the bite was a small nip, at other times a sizable chunk. Dies Lunae, the Roman "day of the moon," became Monandag. The English shortened the name to Monday. The Swedish call it Mandag. The French call it Lundi, from Dies Lunae. In Poland Monday has a quite different origin: there it is called Poniedzialek, "the day after not working."

Roman astrologers named the day after Monday Dies Martis, the day of Mars, the god of war. The red color of the planet Mars made people think of the bloodshed of war.

Tiu, the bravest of the Teutonic gods, was often associated with war, so the Latin Dies Martis became the Teutonic Tiusday. In England the day of Tiu is Tuesday; in Sweden it is Tisdag. In addition to being brave, Tiu was also god of the *ding*, the governing group of the Teutons. In Germany, where Tuesday is called Dienstag, this ancient connection of Tiu with the *ding* persists even today. The Dutch call the day Dinsdag.

MERCURY   DIES MERCURII

In mythology and astrology, gods often have several functions at once or their functions change over the years. For example, the day after Tuesday was called Dies Mercurii, the day of the planet Mercury. Mercury was the messenger of the gods. The planet was the fastest moving and so was especially suited to be a messenger.

The Teutons called the day for Woden (the wind), which also moved very fast. The fit was not exactly right, however, because Woden was an important god, not merely a messenger. In fact, the Teutons made Woden more and more important. He became the Teutonic god of wisdom and the god of poetry and magic. Gradually he was considered the most important god of all.

Wodensdag became Wednesday in English; the Dutch people call it Woensdag. The week begins on Sunday and ends on Saturday, so Wednesday is the middle of the week. Today the German people call it Mittwoch. The Greeks call it Tetarti, the fourth day.

The Romans named the next day Dies Jovis, after the god Jove (Jupiter). Thor was the Teutonic god most like Jupiter, and so the day was called Thorsdag.

Both Jupiter and Thor were gods of thunder and strength. During thunderstorms, Thor rode through the clouds in a wagon pulled by prancing goats and carried a magic hammer in his gloved hands. He hurled it through the air, making a blinding flash.

Thor was thought to bless marriages, so if a thunderstorm occurred during a wedding, it was a sign of good luck.

In England Thor became Thur, and so we have Thursday. The Swedish people call the day Torsdag. The Greeks call it Pempti, meaning the fifth day of the week.

Friday is day number six. The Romans called it Dies Veneris, the day of the planet Venus. The Teutons called it Frigg's day. The Teutons called Frigg by other names: Frigga, Frija, Freya, or Fria. As the wife of Woden, the great god, she was the goddess of married women and mothers as well as a goddess of medicine.

Freitag is the present German word for Friday. The people of Portugal call it Sexta-Feira, the sixth day.

Friday has often been considered the day of bad luck, perhaps because it was the day Jesus was crucified — or, perhaps, because it used to be the day when prisoners were hanged.

To the Romans, Saturday, the day after Friday, was Dies Saturni, the day of the planet Saturn. Saturn was the outermost of all the planets; it traveled most slowly across the sky. Saturn was the Roman god of farming and planting.

The Teutons were not farmers and had no similar god. Instead, they adapted the Roman word to their own language and called the day Saeternesdag.

In Italy, farming was very important. Saturn was

originally the god of planting, and the name came from *satus,* the Latin word for "seed." Saturn was celebrated through much of the year. Eventually a special celebration called the Saturnalia was held for several days around the beginning of winter. For months the sun had been getting lower and lower in the sky. The start of winter marked the time that the sun began to once again move higher in the sky. It would continue this movement for six months, so there was ample reason for rejoicing.

In the early days, a lot of water used to be heated on Saturday nights because that was bath night. The tradition of the Saturday night bath began two thousand years ago. The early Romans believed that the

64

sun was made of fire. Since water is the enemy of fire, you must not wash on the sun's day. But the Romans wanted to wash every day of the week. They solved the problem by washing at night on Saturdays. The Teutons took up the custom, and so did other people. Today, in Iceland, Saturday is called Laugardagur, which means "bath day."

In England, the Teutonic Saeternesdag became simply Saturday. The Dutch call it Zaterdag.

The names of our days of the week therefore have a long history. Sunday, Monday, and Saturday, and all the rest, were based on the seven objects that appeared to move around the earth, all of them visible to the ancient skywatchers. Had they known about the other planets — Uranus, Neptune, and Pluto — our week might now have three more days. We might have had a 10-day week and 36 weeks in a year instead of the 52 weeks we now have.

11. What Is the First Day of the Week?

For most people throughout the world, Monday is the day that starts the week. It's the day we go back to school or back to work after a one- or two-day weekend.

However, according to our calendar, the week begins on Sunday, and Monday is the second day. In fact, the people of Portugal call it Segunda-Feira, the second day.

The order of the days began with the astrologers, the fortune-tellers who were often the astronomers of early times. They observed the planets, the sun, and the moon, and the manner in which they moved. They believed that the earth stood still and that the planets moved around the earth. As they moved, the planets changed position among the stars. The astrologers reasoned that the farthest object must be the one that moved the most slowly. So Saturn must be the farthest of all, for it took about 30 years to complete a journey. Jupiter was somewhat faster, taking about 11 years. Mars took close to 2 years; the sun 1 year. Then came Venus, Mercury, and the moon, all of which took less than a year.

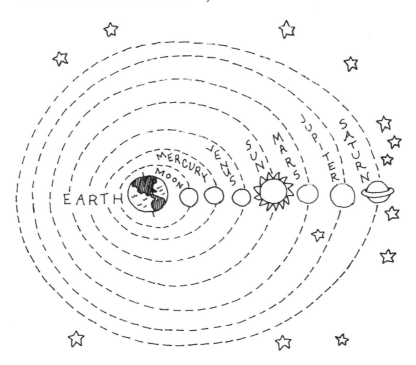

To tell a person's fortune, astrologers began with the day a person was born. To be more accurate, they also wanted to know the hour of that day. The day and the hour were important because each day and hour was related to a particular god. The astrologers believed that the gods determined the events that would occur in a person's life.

Astrologers called the first hour of the first day, our present 7:00 A.M., the sun's day and hour. The sun had that honor because of its importance in bringing warmth to the world. The sun god was Apollo, a most powerful god. The entire day took the name of that first hour.

According to their speeds, the order of the planets was from Saturn, the slowest, to Jupiter, Mars, Sun, Venus, Mercury, and Moon.

Following this order, the hour after the sun's hour was the hour of Venus. The third hour was that of Mercury, then those of the moon, Saturn, Jupiter, and Mars. The eighth hour was once again the sun's hour, and so it went through the 24 hours of the day. The twenty-fourth hour was Mercury's. As you can see from the order of these seven objects, the next object after Mercury is the moon. The day following Sunday was the moon's day. The chart shows the order of the hours of the day and how, every 24 hours, a new day began — one that was devoted to another of the seven planets or gods.

So, as is true of so many of our ideas about time,

the order of the days of the week comes from ancient people. Astrologers put the planets and the days in order so that they could forecast futures more accurately — or so they believed. Chances are, most ancient people had no idea why Monday followed Sunday. They simply accepted the idea and learned to live with it. You and I do exactly the same thing today.

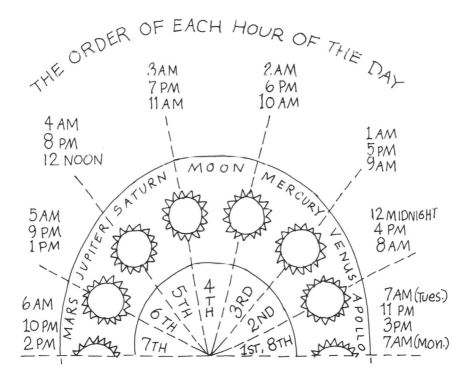

ONE DAY IS 24 HOURS

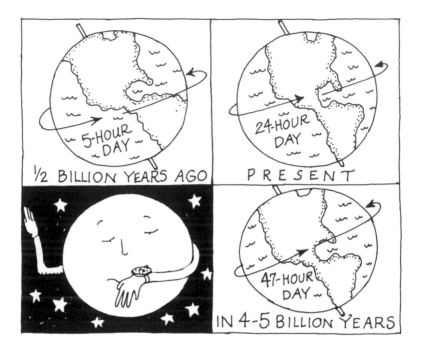

½ BILLION YEARS AGO

5-HOUR DAY

PRESENT

24-HOUR DAY

IN 4-5 BILLION YEARS

47-HOUR DAY

12. Are Days Getting Longer?

A day is the time it takes the earth to make one rotation, about 24 hours. The distance around the earth's equator is close to 25,000 miles. Therefore, the speed of the earth's rotation at the equator is about 1000 miles an hour. That's what it is right now. Some one and a half billion years ago, a day was only five hours long because the earth rotated much more rapidly than it does now. It has been slowing down steadily; every century days get 0.0016 (sixteen ten-thousandths) of a second longer.

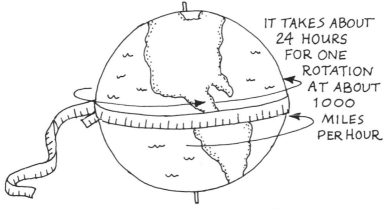

IT TAKES ABOUT 24 HOURS FOR ONE ROTATION AT ABOUT 1000 MILES PER HOUR

CIRCUMFERENCE OF THE EARTH = 25,000 MILES

The earth slows down because of the drag caused by the moon. The differences in the gravitational force of the moon on various locations on the earth cause tides. The water in the oceans and larger seas is always moving, rubbing together, and washing along the shore. These movements produce friction, which takes energy from the earth's rotation. This loss of energy causes the earth to slow down. Its speed drops, and so days become longer.

THE MOON CAUSES TIDES THAT SLOW DOWN THE EARTH

Sixteen ten-thousandths of a second in 100 years isn't much time, but the effect is continuous, so year after year the amount adds up. Four or five billion years from now (if the earth lasts that long), this slowing-down will mean that the earth will take 47 days to rotate once; a day then will be as long as 47 of our present days. The same halves of the earth and moon will always face one another. From the earth, the moon will seem not to rotate, and from the moon, the earth will also seem to be motionless.

This slowing-down will take place over several billions of years. Perhaps a 47-hour day will never be reached, for it is expected that the earth and the moon will last only about five billion years. During our lifetimes, sixteen ten-thousandths of a second in a century won't make any difference.

It is true that you may fool all the people some of the time; you can even fool some of the people all the time; but you can't fool all of the people all the time.
— Lincoln

13. When and Where Does Each Day Begin?

There is a place on the earth where you can have one foot in Monday and the other in Tuesday. That may be hard to believe, but it is true. The place is along the International Date Line, a line that runs through the middle of the Pacific Ocean, from the North Pole to the South Pole.

All around the earth, meridian lines run from pole to pole. On most maps there are 24 of them. The line that goes through Greenwich, England, is called the zero meridian. The next line west of it is the 15-

degree meridian, the next is 30, then 45, 60, and so on. A line is drawn for every change of 15 degrees. During 1 hour, the earth turns through 15 degrees, for a total of 360 degrees (one complete turn) in 24 hours.

The International Date Line follows the 180th meridian, the one that is halfway around the world from Greenwich, England.

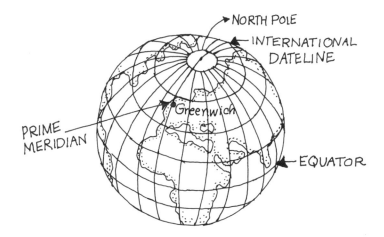

A day must begin somewhere. It was decided that a good place is along the 180th meridian, for it is located in a place where there are few landmasses and therefore very few people. Each day begins and ends at midnight on that line. Suppose it is 12:00 noon on Tuesday at the zero meridian. Fifteen degrees west of Greenwich, the time is 11:00 A.M.; at 30 degrees it is 10:00 A.M., and so on. The time is 1 hour earlier for each change of 15 degrees west. At 180 degrees, the time is 12 hours earlier; it is 12:00 midnight on Monday.

Let's go back to Greenwich, to the zero meridian. Now move eastward. For each change of 15 degrees, the time is 1 hour later. So, at the 180th meridian, the time is 12 hours later: it is 12:00 midnight on Tuesday.

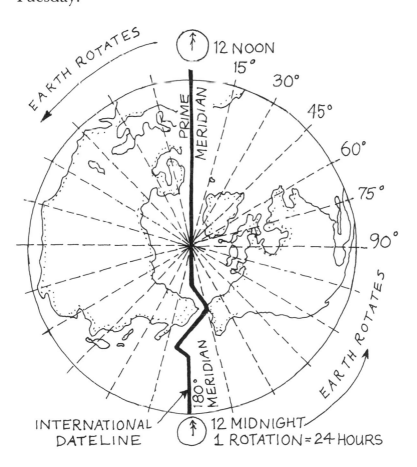

The one location has two different times: midnight on Monday and midnight on Tuesday. If you could straddle the line, it would be Monday for one foot and Tuesday for the other foot.

If you were traveling east at that moment, your clock would show 12:00 midnight on Tuesday. As you crossed the line, your time would be changed to Monday. You would repeat a day.

If you were traveling west, your clock would show midnight on Monday. As you crossed the line, it would become midnight on Tuesday. You would lose a day.

A day is the time it takes the earth to make one rotation. Suppose you are out in space and able to watch the earth turn. When the 180th meridian is beneath you, a new day begins — Tuesday, let us say.

As every other part of the earth passes beneath you it is Tuesday. When the 180th meridian comes around again, the day becomes Wednesday. At that moment, some parts of the earth would be Wednesday while it is still Tuesday west of the meridian.

By using an orange for the earth and a strip of newspaper, you can see why this is so.

THE ☆ INTERNATIONAL DATELINE

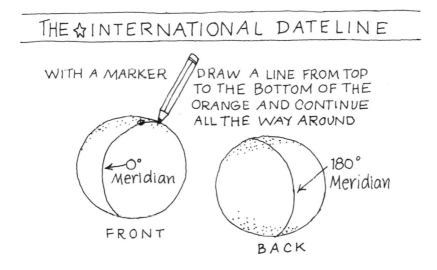

WITH A MARKER DRAW A LINE FROM TOP TO THE BOTTOM OF THE ORANGE AND CONTINUE ALL THE WAY AROUND

0° Meridian

FRONT

180° Meridian

BACK

CUT A STRIP OF NEWSPAPER ½-INCH WIDE

↕ ½"

AND LONG ENOUGH TO GO AROUND THE ORANGE 4 TIMES (ABOUT 32 inches)

MARK THE STRIP INTO 4 EQUAL PARTS

← ABOUT 8" →

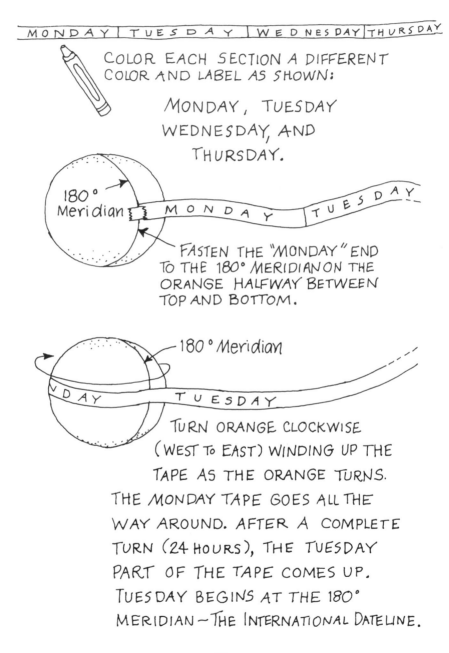

MONDAY | TUESDAY | WEDNESDAY | THURSDAY

COLOR EACH SECTION A DIFFERENT
COLOR AND LABEL AS SHOWN:

MONDAY, TUESDAY
WEDNESDAY, AND
THURSDAY.

180°
Meridian

MONDAY   TUESDAY

FASTEN THE "MONDAY" END
TO THE 180° MERIDIAN ON THE
ORANGE HALFWAY BETWEEN
TOP AND BOTTOM.

180° Meridian

NDAY   TUESDAY

TURN ORANGE CLOCKWISE
(WEST TO EAST) WINDING UP THE
TAPE AS THE ORANGE TURNS.
THE MONDAY TAPE GOES ALL THE
WAY AROUND. AFTER A COMPLETE
TURN (24 HOURS), THE TUESDAY
PART OF THE TAPE COMES UP.
TUESDAY BEGINS AT THE 180°
MERIDIAN—THE INTERNATIONAL DATELINE.

78

As you continue turning the orange, part of it is covered by the Monday strip and part by the Tuesday strip. In some places in the world it is Monday while elsewhere it is Tuesday. Keep turning the orange; Monday will be gone, Wednesday will begin; and so on, day after day.

MONDAY

TUESDAY

THE DATELINE IS THE LAST LOCATION ON THE EARTH TO USE THE OLD DAY AND THE FIRST PLACE TO USE THE NEW DAY.

Remember that time is money.
— Franklin

14. Why Are There Twelve Months in a Year?

The words *month* and *moon* look much the same. They appear to be related — and they are.

Anything that moves in a regular fashion can be used to keep track of time. The earth turns at a steady rate. In ancient times, a day was the time needed for the earth to spin around once, and it still is.

The ancient skywatchers also knew that the sun changed position among the stars. The time needed for the sun to move all around the sky was one year.

People had a short time period — a day — and a long time period — a year. They needed something longer than a day and shorter than a year, so they looked to the moon.

They knew that the moon changed slowly. First it was a thin sliver. After a few days it became a quarter moon. Then it was full. After that, the moon became smaller. It became a quarter moon, then it disappeared from the sky. For a night or so it would not be seen. When next the moon appeared, it was again a thin sliver, a new crescent moon.

A MONTH OF MOONS

The priests of early civilizations watched the evening sky for the first appearance of a new crescent moon. When they saw it, they declared that a new month had begun.

The time needed for the moon to go through these changes was 29½ days — one month.

The changing moon made it possible to divide the year into moons, or months. Since each month was 29½ days long, there would be a bit more than 12 months in a year. Twelve times 29½ gives 354 — 11 days shorter than our present year. To make up the difference, every few years an extra month was added.

The Egyptians said that the moon made a cycle of changes in 30 days, not 29½. Their year also had 12 months. When 12 is multiplied by 30, the result is 360. To make the numbers add up to 365, the number of days in a year, the Egyptians added five special days of celebration to the end of the year. There was no need to add a month, as some people had done.

In the days of early Rome the year had only ten months. It began with March and ended with December. The word December comes from *decem*, which is Latin for "ten." In about 500 B.C., two months were added: January and February. Later, these two extra months were shifted; January became the first month of the year and February the second.

When Julius Caesar became the ruler of Rome, the calendar was out of step with the seasons. The winter months were occurring in autumn, and the autumn months came during the hot days of summer.

The problem developed because a year is not 365 days long; it is 365¼ days. (Actually, it is 365 days, 5 hours, 48 minutes, and 46 seconds.) That's how long it takes the earth to go around the sun.

Another calendar problem arose because 365 cannot be divided evenly by 12. So the months cannot all be the same length.

In Caesar's calendar, the length of the months varied from 28 to 31 days, just as they still do. Four of the months had 30 days, one of them had 28, and the rest had 31. They added up to 365:

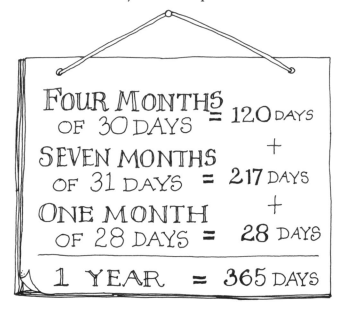

FOUR MONTHS
OF 30 DAYS = 120 DAYS
+
SEVEN MONTHS
OF 31 DAYS = 217 DAYS
+
ONE MONTH
OF 28 DAYS = 28 DAYS
——————————————————
1 YEAR = 365 DAYS

But there are nearly 365¼ days in a year. Something had to be done; otherwise, after another few hundred years, the months of autumn would again be occurring in summer.

It was decided that a day would be added every fourth year. When that was done, the year was called a leap year. This is why. Usually the days in a year follow in order, year after year. If your birthday is on Tuesday this year, it will be on Wednesday next year. But in a leap year it will be on Thursday. The calendar "leaped" over a day. (This is true only if your birthday comes after February 29.)

Adding a day kept the calendar in step with the seasons, and the system worked for several hundred years. But by the 1500s, the calendar was 11 days out of step with the sun's position. To correct the problem, Pope Gregory XIII changed the way we put extra days into the year. See the Gregorian calendar, in the next chapter.

We still use months as big parts of a year. But a month no longer begins with a crescent moon, as it did long ago. The phases of the moon can occur at any time during a month. Look at a calendar and you will see that this is so.

15. The Gregorian Calendar

The Gregorian calendar is used in most of the world. It came about because in 1582, under Pope Gregory XIII, calendar problems that had persisted for centuries were finally solved.

A calendar is a device for recording time. Year after year sky events, such as the beginning of spring, occur on or around the same calendar day.

Calendars were not always able to agree with sky events because, with 365¼ days, a year does not have an even number of days. That quarter of a day causes problems.

In 46 B.C., Julius Caesar decreed that every fourth year there would be an extra day, making that year 366 days long. That should keep things straight.

And it did. But by A.D. 730, the calendar had become a week out of step with sky events. At that time an English monk, the Venerable Bede, figured out that by adding a day every four years, the Julian calendar was adding 11 minutes and 14 seconds too much. Every 128 years the error amounted to one full day. But for centuries nothing was done, and the error became greater. More than 800 years later, in 1582, it was noted that the calendar was 11 days out of step with sky events. Pope Gregory solved the problem by saying that the day after October 4, 1582, should be called October 15, 1582. Also, to keep the

calendar correct over long periods, it was decided that century years would have an extra day only when they could be divided evenly by 400. For example, 1900 was not a leap year, but 2000 will be. The Gregorian calendar would match sky events for thousands of years.

Presently the calendar is kept in step by adding a day every fourth year — the year can be divided evenly by four. Except:

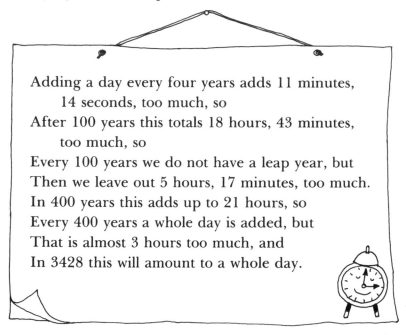

Adding a day every four years adds 11 minutes, 14 seconds, too much, so
After 100 years this totals 18 hours, 43 minutes, too much, so
Every 100 years we do not have a leap year, but
Then we leave out 5 hours, 17 minutes, too much.
In 400 years this adds up to 21 hours, so
Every 400 years a whole day is added, but
That is almost 3 hours too much, and
In 3428 this will amount to a whole day.

Once again an adjustment will have to be made. That year will have a day added because it will be a leap year. And another day because of the accumulated hours.

Many countries adopted the new calendar immediately. The British government and the American colonies did not adopt the calendar until 1752. They said that September 2, 1752, would be called September 14. At the same time it was decided that the year should begin on January 1 and not in March, as had been done for centuries.

Dates had to be shifted about. For example, George Washington's birthday, which had been February 11, 1731 O.S. (old style), became February 22, 1732 N.S. (new style).

The changes were drastic, but the corrections had to be made. Many people resisted, but by 1950 just about all the countries around the world had accepted the new calendar.

1731 FEBR

1	2	3
9	10	11
16	17	18
23	24	25

1732 FEBRUARY

1	2	3	4	5	6
7	8	9	10	11	12	13
14	15	16	17	18	19	20
21	22	23	24	25	26	27
28	☆	☆	☆	☆

16. Time and Space Travel

According to Einstein's theory of relativity, space travelers will not age as fast as people on Earth. The theory has to do with space and time, ideas that are difficult to understand. We think that time passes at the same rate for everyone no matter where they are. But it does not.

However, the speed of light, which is a unit for measuring space and time, is always the same. In every experiment that measures light, the speed is always the same: 186,000 miles a second. That is true whether the measuring instruments are moving toward the light, moving away from it, or standing still. There is no difference.

Suppose there were twins who were 20 years old. One of them stays on Earth for 50 years; the other makes a space journey. When the space traveler returns, he will be 3 or 4 years older, but his twin will be 50 years older. We'll use a train instead of a spaceship to explain why this is so.

A screen is set up at the center of a moving railroad car, and lights are placed at both ends of the car. A bell rings when light from both ends of the car hits the screen at the same instant. Whenever the test is made, whether the railroad car is moving or stopped, the bell rings. It rings because the lights were turned on at the same moment, and the two beams of light traveled the same distance and at the same speed.

TRAIN CAR   screen

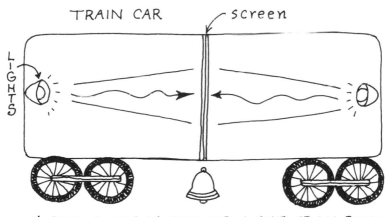

A BELL RINGS WHENEVER LIGHT FROM BOTH ENDS OF THE TRAIN STRIKES THE SCREEN AT THE CENTER.

That's what happens inside the car. If you were outside the car, watching the experiment, you would hear the bell ring, meaning that the light had hit both sides of the screen at the same instant. However, before you heard the bell, it seemed that the two lights were turned on at different times. You saw one light beam traveling forward in the same direction as the train. The other light beam moved in the opposite direction — from the front of the train toward the back.

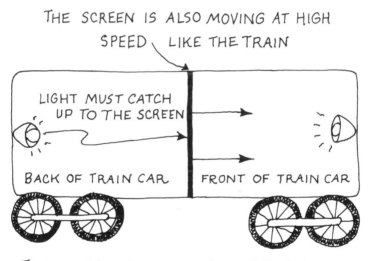

THE SCREEN IS ALSO MOVING AT HIGH SPEED, LIKE THE TRAIN

LIGHT MUST CATCH UP TO THE SCREEN

BACK OF TRAIN CAR   FRONT OF TRAIN CAR

TO AN OUTSIDE OBSERVER OF THE TRAIN TRAVELING AT HIGH SPEED, THE LIGHT TAKES LONGER TO GO TO THE SCREEN FROM THE BACK OF THE CAR THAN FROM THE FRONT.

The first beam had to catch up to the screen. It had to travel more than half the car's length. The second beam, which traveled at the same speed, had to go less than half the length of the car.

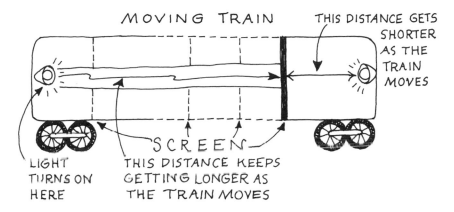

MOVING TRAIN

THIS DISTANCE GETS SHORTER AS THE TRAIN MOVES

LIGHT TURNS ON HERE

SCREEN

THIS DISTANCE KEEPS GETTING LONGER AS THE TRAIN MOVES

But both beams traveled at the same speed. Therefore, the first beam had to start slightly before the second. For a train moving at ordinary speeds, the time difference would be one hundredth of one trillionth of a second.

Clocks inside the train would show that the two beams traveled exactly the same length of time. Clocks outside the train would not.

If the train was moving at close to the speed of light, the first beam would travel thousands of miles before reaching the screen. The other beam would travel a very short distance. So, from your location outside the train, the two events (the giving off of light beams) had to be far apart in time.

Another way to think about these time and distance puzzles is to consider two passengers on another train. They are sitting on opposite sides of the car. The passenger on the far side strikes a match. To the passenger on the near side, the light seems to have come to him straight across the car.

Suppose you are outside the car. As the train goes by, the light seems to travel a longer path before it reaches the second passenger. You see this second passenger move along the track during the interval it takes the light to reach him. At ordinary speeds, the interval would be a small fraction of a trillionth of a second.

If the train were traveling at close to the speed of light, the time difference would be measured in years or decades. For you, outside the train, the two events — the start of the light and its arrival — would be far apart in time. But for the second passenger, the two events would occur at just about the same moment.

This idea was tested by comparing clocks in satellites with clocks on Earth. In every case, the clocks in satellites ran more slowly. The moving clock would be "younger" than the one on Earth.

People have traveled in space during the past several decades, and they will do so throughout the 21st century. They will age more slowly than people who remain on Earth. But they will not be traveling at anywhere near the speed of light, so the age difference will not be apparent.

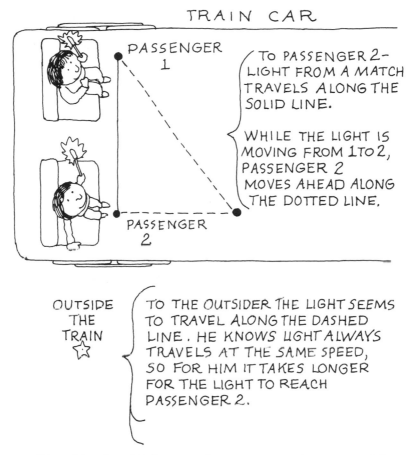

TRAIN CAR

PASSENGER 1

TO PASSENGER 2—
LIGHT FROM A MATCH
TRAVELS ALONG THE
SOLID LINE.

WHILE THE LIGHT IS
MOVING FROM 1 TO 2,
PASSENGER 2
MOVES AHEAD ALONG
THE DOTTED LINE.

PASSENGER 2

OUTSIDE
THE
TRAIN
☆

TO THE OUTSIDER THE LIGHT SEEMS
TO TRAVEL ALONG THE DASHED
LINE. HE KNOWS LIGHT ALWAYS
TRAVELS AT THE SAME SPEED,
SO FOR HIM IT TAKES LONGER
FOR THE LIGHT TO REACH
PASSENGER 2.

Should ultrahigh-speed space travel approaching the speed of light ever be achieved, people aboard the vehicles would be years younger than their counterparts on Earth.

Throughout history, people have dreamed of remaining young; they have searched for "the fountain of youth." Perhaps Einstein found it when he gave us his theory of relativity.

17. Time in Space, on the Moon, and on the Planets

Here on Earth, the rotation of our planet gives us the day, and the revolution of the earth around the sun gives us the year. These motions of the earth regulate our lives. There is a rhythm to our days: a time to get up, to eat, to work and rest, and to go to bed.

If you were on Mars, the rhythm of the days would be about the same, for Mars rotates in just a bit over 24 hours. The year is longer, however, about twice the length of ours.

We would get completely out of rhythm if we were on Mercury. It takes only 88 days for that planet to go around the sun. The time from sunrise to sunrise is 176 Earth days long — the day is twice as long as the year.

Mercury will never be a target for active colonies, but very likely we will eventually have a colony on the moon. There are lunar sunrises and sunsets, but only once a month. Sunrise is followed by two weeks of daylight, and sunset by two weeks of darkness. Human body rhythms could not adjust to the moon's rotation. People would be housed inside a station with controlled conditions, and a regular cycle of changes would be maintained. Lighting would vary as a "day" progressed, simulating changes from dawn to noon, evening, and night. Colonists would follow a daily schedule of eating, exercise, work, relaxing, and sleeping. Without a schedule, the body would not function properly and, chances are, people would become ill and depressed. All of us feel better when we follow a regular routine.

During the relatively short periods that men and women have spent aboard space stations and operated orbital vehicles, artificial sequences of activities have been necessary. For example, the shuttle orbiter experiences several sunrises and sunsets in 24 hours, so body rhythms cannot be tuned to the rising and setting of the sun. Astronauts have various activities to follow in a 24-hour period. All of them are determined by a clock — it tells them to start and stop experiments, chores, and special missions.

Here on Earth we have no such problem. As long as people have lived on our planet, they have more or less regulated their lives by the sun, just as we do today.

We use clocks because they are convenient. A glance gives us the time of day. There is no need to check a sundial or to observe the length and direction of shadows. Also, our clocks work day and night, on cloudy days and sunny, underwater and in dark caves. We have learned to live by the clock.

In the 21st century, people will also live by the clock. But the sun will still be the basis of timekeeping, just as it has been ever since people appeared on the planet.

There's a time for some things, and a time for all things; a time for great things, and a time for small things. — Cervantes

The Sundial

The shadow by my finger cast
Divides the future from the past.
Behind its unreturning line,
The vanished hour no longer thine.

Before it lies the unknown hour
In darkness and beyond thine power.
One hour alone is in thine hands,
The now on which the shadow stands.

Bibliography

Young Readers

Allington, R. *Beginning to Learn About Time*. Milwaukee: Raintree, 1987.

Burns, Marilyn. *This Book Is About Time*. Boston: Little, Brown, 1978.

Fisher, Leonard Everett. *Calendar Art: 13 Days, Weeks, Months, and Years from Around the World*. New York: Macmillan, 1987.

Galt, Tom. *Seven Days from Sunday*. New York: T.Y. Crowell, 1956.

Moscure, Jane. *Wise Owl's Days of the Week*. Chicago: Children's Press, 1981.

Pluckrose, Henry. *Time*. New York: Watts, 1987.

Yoder, Carolyn P., ed. *Faces,* January 1987.

Zubrowski, B. *Clocks: Building and Experimenting with Model Timepieces.* New York: Morrow, 1988.

More Advanced Readers

Boslough, John. "Enigma of Time," *National Geographic,* March 1990, pp. 109–32.

Cynyngham, Henry. *Time and Clocks.* Detroit: Gale, 1970.

Elton, L., and H. Messel. *Time and Man.* New York: Pergamon Press, 1978.

Fraser, J. T. *Time, the Familiar Stranger.* Amherst: University of Massachusetts Press, 1987.

Jesperson, J., and J. Fitz-Randolph. *From Sundials to Atomic Clocks.* New York: Dover.

Price, Arthur. *Past, Present and Future.* New York: Oxford University Press, 1987.

Walker, Roy. *The Time Is Free.* Arden Library, 1989.

Index

104